All Things Unspeakable

Charlotte Leung

BookLeaf Publishing

India | USA | UK

Presentation by *BookLeaf Publishing*

Web: www.bookleafpub.com

E-mail: info@bookleafpub.com

ISBN: 978-93-95755-40-5

First edition 2022

To my dearest readers,

*You may not have been told this today, but you
are enough- you will always be enough.*

How I Wish To Be

The golden canary
who sings by my house all day,
easily find the bright way
always without worry.

You can fly strong and high
above crisp, emerald plains
through violent winds and blue rains
even to heaven's sky.

How I wish to be you
to be loved by all others
with light, sunflower feathers
born with charmed vocals, too.

While I'm the sunken ship
rotting away in deep seas
knowing never to be freed
my beating, dead heart rips.

Unhealthy Note To Self

Don't cry
you must not cry
tears can't solve current problems
emotions aren't real
only spontaneous neural chemical reactions
no one validates vulgar emotional expressions
people won't take a feeler seriously
you must be a stoic, nonchalant individual
even though sometimes you want to cry
waterfalls
while wondering how you still have tears left
to survive society, to survive life
you must not cry
don't cry.

Late Night Showers

A late-night shower-
a small bliss in life.
When my mind nurtures
grim, despairing thoughts
the steaming shower
is where I will sit
and let water drown
my worries away.

Armor

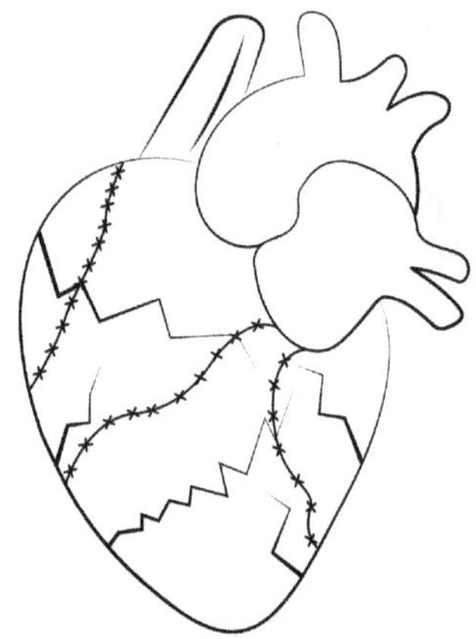

I never curve my lips to a smile
the brave ones say I should smile more
cowards glare from a mile
both of which I decide to ignore.

Very few know it's my diamond armor
wounds cut deep if you are not careful
but I'm unarmed with those of wonder
those who see past my shield, you're special.

Escape

Books are a portal
out of this mundane world
each page turned
makes anxieties vanish
each word fills one
with unfathomable emotions
because readers are with
the characters until the end
that is why
I love books.

Coffee Without Cream and Sugar

Coffee, a ritual almost religious
everyone's saving grace in their morning
for the scholars' overly ambitious
and bakers who wake at the sun's dawning

two creams one sugar, the usual quota
enhances flavors significantly
served in mugs of red, yellow, magenta
waiters rush back and forth ferociously

very rarely is a cup made plain black
few admire its steaming earthy scent
for fatty cream and sweet sugar it lacks
biter black can hardly make one content

piercing bitterness builds resilience
rewards one in fulfilling transience.

Zero

Society orders women to give
patriarchy their utmost devotion
give the system her infinite respect
and two times the respect she shall receive
that is nothing but mocking trickery,
a lie to maintain life of the system
because patriarchy is designed to
only benefit the favored members;
those who are in power stay in power,
unmindful of women, of injustice
no matter how much she gives and obeys,
A million times zero, is zero.

Dancing In the Rain

When inquired,
all say they love the rain
Yet when the sky sheds tears
all open their umbrellas.
Perhaps that is why
I hate to cry
I fear the umbrellas;
weak and shameful- my new labels
umbrellas stay open
when your smile fades into nothing.

I love dancing in the rain
because the sky needs someone who
understands.
Each drop of the sky's pain
will no longer be invalidated.
So find the people
who listen to your every whimper and hurt
find those
whose umbrellas remain untouched
find the ones
who love to dance with you in the rain.

Stronger Together

A pretty thing ribbons are
emerald greens and ruby reds
made of the most luxurious silks
with a few twists and turns
it becomes a bow, star of the show
but with a pull of the fingers
it comes apart
once again, it lingers.

For Those Who Hate Cats

I fear those who say they hate cats
do not understand the concept of love
it's as if love is a chance for control:
they hate it when cats saunter away from their
touch
hate it when cats hiss at them
hate it when cats only leave fur and scratches
they say they love dogs better
because of how immediately affectionate they
are
they fail to understand how cats need personal
space
how cats require patience and mutual trust
how a cat's love has to be earned
they can't see that each cat is stunning and
unique
from the way their tails curl with each step
to the spectrum of striking colors in their eyes
they acknowledge a cat's only purpose is to be
kept as a pet
rather than as a friend, a companion
just as how humans are also made to be a
possession.

Earl Grey

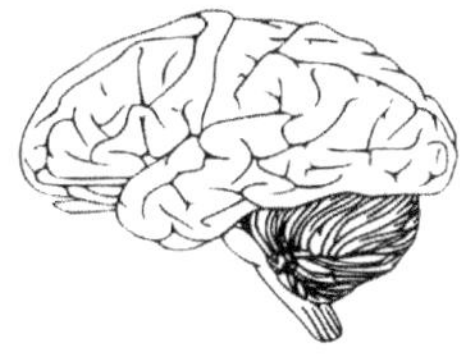

When I have overflowing ideas
a cup of tea is what I'll make
sitting by a window, staring at the endless blue
sky
and let the calming earl grey scent invade every
square inch of air
I dream up magic, madness and maniacal
murder mysteries
for this world is not enough.

Snowflakes

Snowflakes falling in the air
dawning from the clouded blank sky
some so elegant and fair
into white matted sheets they lie

Others dance behind and cry
for too they are also snowflakes
only crumbled up and died
stepped down and dirted at their wake

In this scenery of white
floured treetops and frozen pond
what a magnificent sight
every snowflake flower wanted.

Black

Of all the colorful people in the world
don't be ashamed if your color is black
people of red have hearts of infinite passion
people of orange, gifted with tremendous talent
to create
people of yellow can always transform a frown
into a smile
people of green, the problem solvers, those of
novelty
people of blue can inspire even the most
dejected minds
people of purple hold wisdom from the dawn of
time
people of black may seem like the sidepiece
an accent shade to enhance other vibrant hues
but never forget: black is a mix of all colors.

An Underappreciated Introvert Is A Missing Sock

Socks have a mind of their own
They were made a pair
but destined to be separated.
One sock on each foot,
impossible to cohere in the rhythm of step
tossed into the washer as two
resurfaced in singularity.

At first, one would pay no mind to it
until their favorite pair parts.
Determined to reunite their beloved treasures
one searches frantically around the house.
The sock unwilling to be found
they give up, unaware it lurks in the shadows
giggling madly at the sight of its captor's
hysterical hustle.

Burning Sun

When all hope feels lost,
look to the night sky
notice how each star is just a speck
a white dot nearly diminished by the dark
but really each star is a roaring ball of fire,
gargantuan suns transcended through millennia
hope is never lost
darkness may nearly almost drown you
but you always shine through
because you are a burning sun in this universe.

Highschool Reality

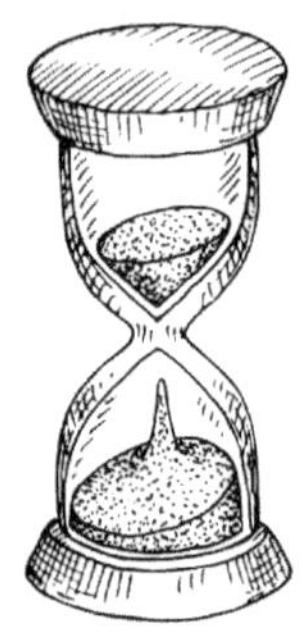

The laughter of friends
and sound of scribbling notes
vanished with a blink.

Until Death Do Us Apart

No man is able to win
against love I have for me
and this love shall never thin
for I shine eternally.

We Are Dreamers

Reality restricts dreamers like us
they lock invisible chains on our wrists
"you must follow the rules, don't make a fuss"
carefree of the anger curled in our fists.

When the stars wake from their restful slumber
we must conjure dreams, escape our prison
flee far away to our sacred harbor
we dare run even when soles bleed crimson.

In this safe haven, we tell tales of old,
ponder innovation, ideas of new
sing and dance, here our chains can't make us
fold
we are true, until birth of morning dew.

Chains tug impatiently, we must leave now
"Until tonight", we swear our sacred vow.